# Go!

*Sharing Jesus Is Easy*

By

Siobhan Livingston

**RB**
Rossendale Books

Kind permission was given by:
Dr. Raymond Wilson, Author of "Jenner of George
Street" Published by Dr. Raymond Wilson in 2000 AD
P.O. Box 485, Mango Hill, QLD, Australia 4509
Email: redowilson@smartchat.net.au

Published by Lulu Enterprises Inc.
3101 Hillsborough Street
Suite 210
Raleigh, NC 27607-5436
United States of America

Published in paperback 2013
Category: Christianity
Copyright Siobhan Livingston © 2013

ISBN : 978-1-291-51734-7

# Dedication

*I dedicate this to you Mum. The world is a brighter place when you are around.*

# Acknowledgements

*David:*
*Thank you for your enduring unending support and for spurring me on to the finish line.*

*Michele:*
*Without your prophetic vision, I would not have seen this booklet coming. God and you began all this!*

*Rosemary, Colm, Pastors John and Hilary, and Karen:*
*Thank you for wading through the lengthy first version! Your encouragement made all the difference.*

*Bangor Community Church:*
*What an amazing church family! Thanks so much to all of you who helped in any way with this booklet.*

*To Vincent in Rossendale Books:*
*You have been a God-send. I deeply appreciate your help in getting this booklet from my computer into the hands of others. Thank you.*

# Table of Contents

*How lovely on the mountains*
*Are the feet of him*
*Who brings good news*
*Who announces peace*
*And brings good news of happiness,*
*Who announces salvation,*
*And says to Zion,*
*"Your God reigns!"*

Isaiah 52:7

# Chapter 1

## It's Easy

*"Lord, help me to see what You want me to see, hear what You want me to hear and do what You want me to do."*

Have you got a minute to spare every day? If you do, you could put that 60 seconds to good use.

One minute. What difference will one minute make?

It can make a huge difference. In fact, it is possible to reach hundreds of people with the Gospel in one year, using one minute a day, every day.

How is this possible?

It's easy - by sharing a seed of the Gospel with one person every day for a year. You could share it at a level you are comfortable with. That may mean you would;

Give a tract to someone.

Tell someone "Jesus loves you" perhaps, while

handing out the tract.

Post a tract through someone's door.

Engage people in conversation and share with them the way of salvation.

Knock on a door to tell people about Jesus.

Or perhaps it may mean a mix of all these different ways.

You could share the good news of Jesus but in a manner of your own choosing. The person you share with doesn't have to be someone you know so the possibilities are limitless!

You can start any day, week or month. If you committed to doing this, in one year you would touch 365 people with the good news of Jesus Christ! One person reaching 100's of souls in one year with very little time or effort required. It only takes seconds to give a tract to someone, or to say, "God has a great plan for your life" to a person. This is something every Christian could get involved with easily and effortlessly. The strategy is to share the Gospel through words, whether written or verbal, daily. The commitment is not to lead a soul to Christ every day, nor is it to invite someone to a Christian gathering. Rather, it is to be faithful in sowing the Word into someone's life every day for one year.  God asks that we play our part in sowing the seed of the Word into hearts so He can bring conviction.

You mingle with more people in a day than you realise; travelling to and from destinations, walking, shopping, queuing, meeting people who come to do work in your house or garden, dropping off/picking up children to/from school, answering so-called "nuisance" phone calls, participating in hobbies or keeping various appointments.  As you can see, you are not limited to people you know.

When a minister friend of mine receives phone calls asking him to participate in a survey or asking him about some sales deal or other, he says to them, *"Can I ask you a question now?"* He then proceeds to share the Gospel with them.  Brilliant!

A man from my church who committed to sharing Jesus once a day for a year phoned a help desk regarding a problem he was experiencing with his television network.  The lady he eventually got talking to noted that he seemed very happy.  Ryan replied, "That's the joy of the Lord."  This opened up a whole conversation about Jesus.  Eventually she asked if she could ring him back after her shift was over to talk more about Jesus.  The end result?  She is now saved and attending a church!

Perhaps there are days when you don't meet people.

What about sending a text or an email to someone? Or posting a tract through a neighbour's door? You could decide to do a house a day until you have posted a tract through your whole neighbourhood, and then move on to do this in another area. Some may purpose to go and knock on a house door and talk to the person who answers about Jesus.

He loves you so much. That is already a done deal. Telling people about Jesus will not make Him love you any more than He already does. He loves you passionately, completely, wholly and unconditionally. This is not an exercise in getting into God's "good books." It's about your lost brothers and sisters who still don't know Jesus. What about them? The whosoever are waiting for someone to show them the way out of their mess. That someone could be you.

An awesome woman of God, Carol Savage, wrote this about Satan's tactics to keep us from going after the lost.

"He (Satan) will do anything to keep you away from a soul that belongs to him. This is still Satan's tact today."

"Give me the souls," (Satan says)... "I'll keep you distracted in your mind with arguments and accusations. I'll whisper condemnations. I'll keep you busy - busy in your home life, busy in your workplace, even busy in your church. I'll distract you with everything. I've had years of practice … but GIVE ME THE SOULS! "

Satan has had years of practice to keep us from going. Look at your own life to see if his tactics have worked. The Great Commission was very simple – go. Jesus put the most important word at the very beginning of the sentence. Go. It's so simple we have almost missed it. We are to go. Where are we to go? Into the world. We are not to be part of the world, but we are to go into it with the good news. Mark 16:15 "And He said to them, Go into all the world and preach and publish openly the good news (the Gospel) to every creature (of the whole human race)." (Amplified Bible)

Paul encouraged Timothy in 2 Tim. 4:5 to endure hardship and do the work of an evangelist. "But you, be sober in all things, endure hardship, do the work of an evangelist, fulfill your ministry." Out of all the good works Paul could have encouraged this young pastor to do, he cited evangelism. He could have said to Timothy, "Do the work of a pastor." Or "Do the work of a teacher." Or "Do the work of an apostle." But no, Paul specifically chose the ministry of the evangelist to emphasise to Timothy. He was saying to him, "Centre your ministry around evangelism. Let soul winning be at the heart of all you do. If you do this, you will fulfil your call." Every person's calling was created to have soul winning at its hub. God may have called you to be a secretary, architect, plumber, waitress, pastor, entrepreneur, prophet, worship leader, mother, father, wife, husband...the list is endless. Be the best you can be at what God has called you to be – and reach the lost while you are doing it.

Your life may not be perfect - whose is? You may think your life is quite the opposite to perfect. You may be going through trials and hardships. Remember Paul said, "Endure hardship. Do the work of an evangelist." God is letting us know here that there will be hardships to overcome. In fact, I believe He was saying that the work of the evangelism will mean enduring and overcoming hardships in order to effectively reach the lost. We mustn't let difficulties become an excuse for not sharing the Gospel. Paul said in 2 Cor. 12:9, 10, "My grace is sufficient for you, for power is perfected in weakness." Most gladly, therefore, I will rather boast about my weaknesses, so that the power of Christ may dwell in me. For when I am weak, then I am strong." And again Paul wrote in 1 Cor. 1:27, "But God has chosen the foolish things of the world to shame the wise, and God has chosen the weak things of the world to shame the things which are strong."

Moses had committed murder and, many believe, he had some kind of speech impediment. Yet he led God's people out of the bondage of Egypt. What was his secret? He knew he couldn't do it in his own physical strength, but he trusted that with God, all things were possible. God promised Moses, "Now then go, and I, even I, will be with your mouth, and teach you what you are to say." Exodus 4:12. Why not make that Scripture your prayer? "Lord, I will go. As I do, I believe that You will be with my mouth and that You will teach me what to say."

A friend of mine, Linda, suffered from a noticeable speech impediment when she was a child. I didn't know her then but met her a few years ago. She has battled many things in her life, including self-harming, low self-image, depression, divorce, and a painful physical disability which requires her (at the moment) to walk using a stick. Do you know this lady has one of the biggest hearts for the lost I have ever seen? She regularly participates in street outreaches. Her heart for people shines through her eyes and her words as she speaks to them about Jesus. Several have been won to the Lord over the years through the faithful ministry of this woman of God. Many of them still come to our church and are growing in their faith.

Linda has truly endured hardship and done the work of the evangelist. She is one who demonstrates the power of God being made perfect in weakness. God's power is able to take over when we are weak because then, it HAS to be Him! So don't see your weaknesses as a liability or something to stop you sharing Jesus. Rather view them, in a sense, as your greatest asset! Allow God to take over and more than make up for any weakness you may feel you have. That way, His perfect power will flow through you each day.

My friend, I hope Linda's story has encouraged you not to wait until your life is a bed of roses before you tell people about Jesus. "Not by might nor by power, but by My Spirit," says the Lord of hosts. Zechariah 4:6. It is not by our own might or strength we witness, but by His. I thank God He is the Great Equaliser. He doesn't disqualify anyone on the basis of their past, their health, their educational achievements, or even their ability to speak. God simply needs willing vessels.

Audrey, another precious lady I know, suffered with very bad eyesight to the point where she couldn't read or properly make out people's faces. (A great healing work is in progress and now her eyesight is almost fully restored). Even before the Lord began to heal her vision, she was faithful to come out every time we did a street outreach. She handed out tracts to people she couldn't see, with such joy in her heart that the Lord had privileged her to labour alongside Him. She blesses me so much. Audrey's way of thinking is that there is nothing to stop her going out to share Jesus with people. What a champion!

I can't move on without mentioning Michael.

Michael loves Jesus. He is a man of few words and battles shyness. The first time he went out knocking on doors to share the Gospel with a team from our church he led a young man to the Lord. Any evangelistic endeavour we arrange, Michael is the first to sign up. I have seen his confidence grow over the years as he has been faithful to reach out with the powerful Gospel of Jesus Christ. Michael didn't let his awkwardness around people hinder him. Instead, he simply obeyed and went. God did the rest.

You and God together can overcome any obstacle. He will empower and strengthen you as you go to tell people about what Jesus has done for them. The most important requirement is that you love God and people. It's God's love shining through your eyes that will change lives as you hand out that tract. I am convinced it is not more knowledge of the Bible we need, but more love. Please hear me. I am NOT saying we don't need to read our Bibles daily and study God's infallible Word. We do. However, I believe if we fell in love with Jesus more than ever, this would result in massive numbers of Christians going into the world to preach the Gospel. Multitudes would be reached and it wouldn't be long before Jesus returned.

More and more those words of Jesus are ringing in my ears. "Behold, I am coming quickly, and My reward *is* with Me, to render to every man according to what he has done." Rev 22:12. And again in verse 20, "He who testifies to these things says, 'Yes, I am coming quickly.' Amen. Come, Lord Jesus." What a glorious day that will be!

It is exciting an adventure once you decide to share Jesus daily. Every delay becomes a Divine appointment. Every coincidental meeting becomes an opportunity. Every trip outside the doors of your home holds the prospect of an open door into someone's life somewhere. Purpose will flood your life as you and God go hand in hand to share His words with people.

On the practical side, set a date to start. Tell a friend. And begin. Find some excellent tracts and keep them stocked up in your home. Every time you go out, make sure you have some with you in a place you can get at easily and quickly. You may find it helpful to hold one in your hand if you are walking somewhere. Always make sure your church's contact details are on the tract.

If necessary, allow yourself some time to build up your evangelism muscles. For the first couple of weeks during your preparation, start to notice people and acknowledge them in a friendly way as you are out and about. Smiling is good, saying "Hello" as you pass with a smile is even better. Or engaging someone you "know to see" in small talk. People are usually very friendly and willing to talk or share a smile. What about beginning to chat to the person at the checkout while shopping? People at checkouts are excellent candidates for your evangelism efforts. They are paid to be nice to you and they aren't going anywhere!

After getting used to being friendly to people as you are out and about for a couple of weeks, perhaps it's time to move forward. Once a week, post a tract through someone's door or give out a tract. Another idea is if the weather is suitable, go to an area where there is outdoor seating and take a seat. If the weather is not good, perhaps try going to some indoor area, like a shopping centre, and take a seat. Ask the Lord to bring the person or people along that He wants to touch with His Word. Begin to chat in a friendly manner to whoever He brings along. In our climate, the state of the weather is always a good conversation opener! At the right time, you could offer them a tract. Or you may want to invite them along to some special event taking place at your church. Inviting people to Christian gatherings at your church or some other venue is not what Go! is about. Go! is about sowing some seed of the Gospel verbally or in written form into someone's life. However in this initial "warm up" stage, it is an excellent way to prepare you for the real task of sharing Jesus. Ask the Lord for creative ways to reach people and He will show you. Begin to exercise your faith by engaging in this kind of evangelism, but only once a week initially.

19

After a short period of time, increase this to twice a week. Then three times a week, and so on until you know you are ready to take on the challenge of sharing Jesus each day for a year. You will find your confidence and boldness growing as you step out in this.

You may decide you need fewer weeks to prepare. The important thing is that you begin. Talking about going is brilliant. However it is only in *doing* it that you fulfil it.

I attended an evangelism course which Crown Jesus Ministries (who are based in Belfast) were running. At one of those meetings, Mitch, (CJM Director) shared with us how he was working upstairs in his office when a knock came to the front door of their ministry premises. He ran down and found it was their window cleaner. Mitch began to chat to him. After a few minutes, he asked him the question, "Are you a Christian?" The young man responded, "No, I'm not." Mitch replied, "Why not?" I can't remember what the man responded on that occasion. However, over a period of time and after several other conversations with Mitch, this man eventually surrendered his life to Jesus.

I praise God for this young man's salvation and for Mitch's faithfulness in reaching out to him. However, the real reason I am including this story is that those two questions changed my evangelistic life! The big deal for me had always been, "How do I bring the conversation around to God?" I don't think I am alone in this. I know many of you are nodding your head as you read. Those two simple questions, "Are you a Christian?" and "Why not?" can be used in any conversation, anywhere and anytime. Try it and see for yourself. It really is that easy.

Many times when I go through various checkouts, I sow some seed of the Word into the person working at the till. I remember the time when I was doing some grocery shopping and I bumped into two precious saints from my church. The Lord nudged me to offer them a lift home, which they accepted. As I had a full trolley of shopping which I still had to pay for, they offered to help me go through the checkout. "Show them how it's done," the Holy Spirit whispered to me. I knew the lift home was an assignment from the Lord only to keep them with me at the checkout. One of them had to sort something else out, so in the end there was one left helping me.

We began to empty my trolley and load the counter. While doing so, I began asking a series of questions to start a conversation with the sales assistant. God certainly has a sense of humour because on that one particular occasion, I met the only sales assistant ever that didn't know they were paid to be nice to the customer! His whole body language was screaming at me, "Back off, I don't want to talk!" It occurred to me I may have actually met a sales person I couldn't crack!

I kept the questions flowing, adding in my own comments here and there. My smile was getting sweeter and sweeter. I was not giving up! Suddenly the breakthrough came. He made eye contact. (Up to that point, the entire conversation had taken place without one bit of eye contact on his part). Straightaway I seized the moment. "Are you a Christian man?" I asked. His guard had dropped and he responded honestly to my question that he wasn't. "Why not?" I asked. From his response, I was able to sow some seed from the Word as the Lord led. (Don't be put off by thinking you may not know the answer to the "Why not?" question. God will show you the simple answer to make.)

There are other occasions when I use different approaches. You may find this helpful. "Has anyone ever told you that God loves you and has a wonderful plan for your life?" Or my personal favourite is, "Have you ever asked Jesus into your heart?" The beauty of either of these two approaches is that no matter how the person responds, you have already sown a seed.

Recently I was with my mum in a Department Store while she was buying some new clothes. There were several sales counters. In order to purchase or make any inquiries regarding any item, you had to go to the relevant counter. We had a lot of queries in our search so I began to talk to each sales clerk in order to gently lead in to sharing the Gospel.

Each conversation opened differently as I felt prompted by the Holy Spirit. One thing I learned in Catholic Ireland was NOT to ask, "Are you a Christian?" This simple question works wonders the majority of times in Protestant circles, but amongst Catholics, it causes bewilderment.

Mum decided to purchase an item. After some small talk with the Sales Assistant, I asked her, "Have you ever asked Jesus to be your Lord and Saviour?" Her eyes locked with mine and I could see she had never heard a question like it before in her life but she wanted to know more. "It's all about a personal relationship with Jesus" I continued. "It's about making Him Boss and Lord over every area of your life."

"That's very interesting. Tell me more," she replied. I began to explain the way of salvation to her while her colleague also listened in, intrigued.

We finished purchasing the item and began to walk away when she started to relate about sicknesses in her life. I felt that familiar Holy Ghost tug. "Would you like me to pray for you?" I asked. Well, one thing led to another and five minutes later, there was a party in Heaven! Mary surrendered her life to Jesus in a heartfelt prayer. She quite happily gave me her full name and contact details and permission to give these details to a local pastor, which I did.

I don't lead a sales assistant to the Lord every time I engage them in conversation. However, I am open to harvesting a soul if there is an obvious candidate in front of me. Whether you lead a person to Jesus or you sow seed, you are playing your part in rescuing people from an eternity in hell. You may find your heart beating rapidly as you start off in this. However God's courage will rise up in you – as well as your joy – as you faithfully undertake this commitment. Jesus' command in Mark 16:15 "Go into all the world and preach the gospel to all creation" is for you to obey too, not just others. Ask yourself honestly, "How much have I been obeying this command?"

# Chapter 2

## A Little Goes A Long Way

*"Nobody made a greater mistake than he who did nothing because he could do a little."* Edmund Burke.

Probably before reading chapter one it had never occurred to you that you could reach hundreds of people in one year by committing to sow the Word into one person's life every day for that year. This is the Go! challenge. If it took you 30 to 60 seconds per day to sow the Word, it would mean for 15 minutes to half an hour of your time each month, you would reach 365 people in a year. That's what I call a worthwhile investment!

What if a friend decided to join you in this challenge? At the end of the year, 730 people would be touched with the Gospel of Jesus Christ. If three of you joined together to do this, the number would be 1095! Three people reaching over 1000 souls - *over 1000 souls!!* - without much cost, effort or time. Multitudes of evangelistic outreaches have expended a lot in terms of time, effort and cost to reach far less. Go! enables you and your friends, within the borders of your lifestyle, to easily and effortlessly share Jesus.

If a group of seven decided to take up the challenge they would reach 2,555 people. In Belfast the Waterfront Hall seats 2,500 people. That's a large building. To hire it out, pay for advertising, insurances and everything else that goes with putting on an outreach of this scale, costs would easily go into thousands of pounds. However, seven people can reach 2,555 people with no stress and for minimal cost.

Pastor, church leader – would you consider operating Go! in your church? If 20 people got involved, they would reach 7,300 people in one year. That's a serious number of people. That's the equivalent of holding three big crusades in the Waterfront Hall in one year. Even accounting for some people being reached several times by the group of 20, their numbers would still be in the thousands! The effect of hearing the Gospel several times is faith. Faith comes by hearing and hearing and hearing the Word. God knows who He is targeting in any given season. He knows where it's at with each person and He knows how to reach them. However He needs your availability. *Are you available?*

| 12 MONTH PERIOD | | |
|:---:|:---:|:---:|
| (One person per day) | | |
| **No. Sharing** | | **No. Hearing** |
| 1 | | 365 |
| 2 | | 730 |
| 3 | | 1095 |
| 4 | | 1460 |
| 5 | | 1825 |
| 6 | | 2190 |
| 7 | | 2555 |
| 8 | | 2920 |
| 9 | | 3285 |
| 10 | | 3650 |
| 20 | | 7300 |
| 30 | | 10950 |
| 40 | | 14600 |
| 50 | | 18250 |

*Chapter 3*

## Rescue!

A large cruise liner lit up the night sky. This liner had the best the world could offer - swimming pools, restaurants, shops, theatres, night clubs, bars and casinos were all in good supply. Multitudes of people were on board this liner savouring its delights. One day in deep waters, a violent storm arose. The liner was buffeted from side to side. Finally it succumbed and sunk to a watery grave.

As far as the eye could see, souls were screaming for help as waves swelled all around. A mayday message had been picked up by a Life Saving Ship, the *JC International*. As soon as the call for help was received, the *JC International* set course to get there as fast as it could. Upon arrival, what a scene its crew beheld! Straight away, the rescue operation began.

As well as a Life Saving Ship, the *JC International* was also a training ship. People signed up and were trained in the various aspects of water rescue. It was on-the-job training. As soon as a new conscript arrived, they were immediately sent out to rescue people. They had discovered this was the best way to train. If a conscript was taught a lot of theory with

28

no practical application, many lost interest in the real job of rescuing people and became comfortable in just learning theory. Included amongst the new trainees were many who had actually signed up years ago to be a part of the *JC International's* rescue operations. For various reasons though, they had failed to turn up for duty. They were on board today as a result of a fresh recruiting campaign and were eager to begin their new life of adventure.

The other reason why conscripts were immediately sent out was the great need. Cruise liners were sinking. People were dying due to lack of rescue workers. It was all hands on deck. On board were deep sea divers, long distance swimmers, helicopter airlift rescue operators and life boat rescue teams. Through their skilful endeavours, many had been saved.

Despite these highly trained rescue workers working at maximum capacity, they couldn't get to the majority of the drowning people without more help – and lots of it. Most on board the ship were new conscripts. Only that morning, many had signed up. They set sail from the harbour embarking on a new life aboard the *JC International* just a few hours earlier. A crackling noise came through the ship's intercom system. "This is your Captain speaking. All hands on deck. I repeat - all hands on deck." The new conscripts ran to the decks, located the rings and began throwing them. Soon the sea was awash with people clinging to these precious lifelines. **Because of their prompt action, many lives that otherwise would have been lost, were saved that day.** The rings kept people afloat long enough for one of the other rescue workers to achieve a full rescue. A successful mission! Not one lost!

This story is about the Church and the world. The *JC International* is the Church. The cruise liner is the world. Its occupants don't have a personal relationship with Jesus and are seduced and preoccupied by the world's delights. They have built their lives on sandy foundations and are oblivious to their need of a Saviour. However, when storms hit, their lives crumble. In the water, desperate to stay alive, we see a picture of the multitudes of lost souls destined for hell.

The training technique the *JC International* used was to send new conscripts out immediately to rescue people. This is a picture of new believers being trained straight away to share their faith openly. The *JC International* had found that if they didn't send them out straight away, they became comfortable and more interested in learning about rescue than actually doing it. This represents what happens in the Church. How many are more comfortable talking about sharing their faith and studying about evangelism, than actually doing it? Too many. We leave it to others. "It's not up to me" we think and close our mouths. "That's not my ministry" we say and remain silent.

I can't help but think about what happened as the *Titanic* disappeared below the water. While the screams of those drowning all around them filled the air, many half filled lifeboats sat a short distance away. This makes sobering thinking. Your life is a lifeboat. You may feel you don't know enough to save anyone. The truth is, if you know Jesus, you know enough. From the moment of your new birth, you were equipped to rescue the lost.

Many say "I'm not an evangelist." They are probably correct. Not everyone is an evangelist. But every believer *is* called to evangelise. In fact, it is our birth right as a child of God. We have the privilege of telling others about Jesus. We are duty bound to do so. 2 Corinthians 5:17-20 talks about believers having the ministry of reconciliation. The evangelist's function is to train and equip believers to evangelise. Not everyone is called to train and equip. But everyone is called to evangelise. Proverbs 24:11,12a says, "Rescue the perishing; don't hesitate to step in and help. If you say, "Hey, that's none of my business," will that get you off the hook?" THE MESSAGE. I know if you are reading this manual, you are not looking for excuses to get out of sharing your faith. Rather, you have a growing desire to find opportunities to tell people they are forgiven!

Who will rescue the lost? Who will save them? Who will tell them about Jesus – your pastor? Praise God for your pastor. He's highly skilled and can be compared to one of the deep sea divers. He knows how to reach people who have fallen to great depths. However the harvest is too great for your pastor.

Who will help him - the apostle, the prophet and the teacher? They could be likened to the long distance swimmers. They know how to minister the Word to reach the lost. However, the harvest is too great for them.

Who will help them - the evangelist? Ah yes, surely the evangelist will get the job done? He could be likened to the air rescue operator. He knows how to share the Good News in ways that reach those outside Christ. However, the harvest is too great even for the evangelist.

Who will help him - faithful mature Christians, and those serving God in some ministry capacity? What would we do without them? They can be compared to the lifeboat teams fearlessly braving every obstacle to rescue another soul from Satan's grip. Their expert explanation of the way of salvation brings conviction on hearts and many Christians are birthed. However, the harvest is still too great for them. **Even with the combined efforts of all the apostles, prophets, evangelists, pastors,** teachers, **faithful mature Christians and all those serving God in some ministry capacity – the harvest is still too great.** That's why Jesus (the Captain of the ship) is calling for **all** hands on deck. The deep sea divers, long distance swimmers, air rescue experts and lifeboat people were all working flat out and still couldn't get to the multitudes of people who were drowning. Without the immediate action of the new conscripts disaster would have been inevitable. Many lives would have been lost had the ring throwers not responded to that call.

Who are these ring throwers? We called them "new conscripts." They represent people who recently accepted Christ as their Lord and Saviour. The new conscripts also represent those who had surrendered their lives to Christ quite a while ago, but had not grown in their faith. Perhaps the lies of the devil had convinced them for whatever reason that they weren't "worthy" to be part of their Lord's Life Saving Team. They felt inadequate to share their faith. Some have been way laid by sickness, family problems, crisis after crisis, a feeling of inferiority, fear, complacency, shyness and embarrassment. They came from all backgrounds. Many wrongly believed their part was to do nothing and let the preachers do all the work. Fear was a big issue. The thoughts of talking to anyone and telling them about Jesus terrified most. This story relates how a new day had dawned for them. They realised how vital they were to the success of the rescue mission and responded with action.

In Matthew 9:37 (NKJV), Jesus said to His disciples, "The harvest truly is plentiful, but the labourers are few." Jesus' own words are "the labourers are few." In other words there are only a few people setting about to bring in the massive harvest. It is estimated that the combined number of apostles, prophets, evangelists, pastors and teachers today make up only 2% of the Body of Christ worldwide. How are 2% of Christians going to reach the worldwide harvest that needs to be brought in? God needs the other 98% to mobilise and harvest also! That's why Jesus went on to say, "Therefore beseech the Lord of the harvest to send out workers into His harvest" (verse 38. NAS).

**Maybe you are not a deep sea diver, long distance swimmer, air rescue or lifeboat operator. But you could be a ring thrower.** You can throw a ring by carrying a bundle of excellent tracts in your bag or jacket pocket and giving one to someone today. Perhaps as you gain confidence, you could say something like, *"Jesus loves you"*, or *"Jesus cares for you"* while handing out the tract. It's as simple as that. Who knows the far-reaching consequences of that tract, that word, that short conversation?

When I was 17, I was waiting with my friends to catch the bus home after school one afternoon. A badge one of my friends was wearing caught my eye. To this day, the words on that badge comfort me. It simply said, "Jesus Cares." I never said anything to Colette (my friend who was wearing it), but now, I can still visualise that badge and I can still see those words. I remember that moment often. A seed was sown in my heart that is still bearing fruit today. I'm sure Colette didn't realise the far- reaching impact her badge would have on my life, so much so that I would write about it in a booklet many years later. Two words – one sentence. That was all I needed that day. Sometimes it only takes two words to change someone's world.

1 Cor. 3:6 says, "I planted, Apollos watered, but God all the while was making it grow and He gave the increase," (Amplified Bible). Seeds cannot grow unless they are planted. Have you ever seen seed grow into plants while they stayed in the packet? Of course not! First they have to be planted before there is any possibility of them growing.

Colette planted a seed in my life that was watered many times by faithful saints. But it was God Who made it grow and increase. In the same way we don't understand how a baby is formed in the womb. Once that seed is sown in a woman, God takes that seed and breathes His life into it. Forming, shaping, multiplying, growing and increasing it all the while. So too it is with the Word of God. First it needs to be sown. Once it has been planted in someone's heart, God watches and hovers over it, breathing His life into it. He leads others to water that seed with His Word and love. It's His work. He is "making it grow and become greater," (1 Corinthians 3:7, Amplified Bible).

Giving someone a tract or telling someone that God is not mad at them, but mad about them, may seem like a small thing to do. It may seem like an insignificant task because it is so easy. Just because something is easy, doesn't make it unnecessary. This is an hour in history, as never before, when God is requiring ring throwers to throw life saving rings.

Our part is to believe the Word enough to do it.

From then on the rest is up to Him.

# Chapter 4

## You Are An Important Link

Frank Jenner was a man in Sydney Australia who coined a sentence he used hundreds of times – with far reaching results. For years he approached people with the question, *"If you were to die tonight, where would you be, in Heaven or in Hell?"* [1] In England, a pastor met a man who had received Christ because of his encounter with Mr. Jenner. Mr. Jenner had asked him this question, *"If you were to die tonight, where would you be, in Heaven or in Hell?"* Interestingly, that same summer of 1953, this pastor heard another man's story. This man also eventually became a Christian through meeting the Australian sailor. When Francis Dixon, the pastor, went to Australia, he met two other men who also had similar stories. They had each met a man in Sydney who had asked them *"If you were to die tonight, where would you be, in Heaven or in Hell?"* Both had come to Christ because of meeting Mr. Jenner as they passed by him on the street. Frank Jenner had been a vital link in the chain that had led to each of them surrendering their lives to God.

---

[1] Dr. Raymond Wilson *Jenner of George St* (QLD, Australia: Dr. Raymond Wilson, 2000), p. 51).

Frank Jenner didn't realise the impact his efforts were having for 16 years. Francis Dixon decided to track him down in Sydney and told him about how four of the people he had asked his pertinent question to had gone on to serve God. When Jenner heard this, he fell down on his knees and cried, *"O Lord, thank You for toleratin' me."* [2]

After that visit to Mr. Jenner's house, Francis Dixon went on to hear of a further seven people (making it a total of 10) who had all come to faith as a result of their encounter with Mr. Jenner. I wonder how many others there are?

Dr. Raymond Wilson writes that *"Jenner himself never occupied a prominent position in his church or in Christian service. His gifts were those of a good personal worker. He was not a platform man. Never once was he asked to preach in his own Assembly, and never once did he seek the public place. He worked humbly and unobtrusively behind the scenes. But those whom God saved through his ministry did in many cases go on to fill positions of spiritual responsibility and to serve God in the wider public sphere. This was true of the first four "Jenner-men" whom Francis Dixon "discovered". Peter Culver, Noel Stanton, Murray Wilkes, and the man from Perth. All became well known evangelists themselves. Peter Culver is still active in an itinerant Bible-teaching ministry. Noel Stanton is a powerful Gospel preacher and Murray Wilkes, with his wife, for many years conducted evangelistic camps throughout Australia for young*

---

[2] Wilson p. 54

*people. All these men possessed gifts that Frank Jenner did not have. God took up Frank Jenner, the one-talent man, and multiplied that one talent many times in the lives of others."* [3]

Frank Jenner would have been the first person to tell you he was not an evangelist. One Christian brother who was in the same church as Frank Jenner, on hearing this story, expressed surprise and said words that went something like this, *"…he couldn't preach, in fact I didn't think he would be much good at anything."* [4] Dr. Wilson writes, *"It is sad that for most of his life, the true value of Jenner's work went unrecognised."* [5] Mr. Jenner approached people with his single-sentence sermon for 16 years before he heard about any lasting fruit in the lives of the people he had talked to. What was his secret? It was his willingness to be a link in the chain. *"There are often many links in the chain of soul winning. Jenner was in many cases only a link, albeit an important one. Some laboured before him, others followed after to complete God's work in the soul."* [6] *The important thing is that none of us should be a "missing link" in the chain."* [7]

What an example for us! Here was a man who apparently didn't have a preaching or teaching gift. He held no prominent position in church. He was no great orator. And yet it would be hard to

---

[3] Wilson p. 86
[4] Wilson p. 84
[5] Wilson p. 84
[6] Wilson p. 84
[7] Wilson p. 86

calculate the thousands of lives his life impacted for God, not only in Australia but in nations beyond. (Dr. Wilson gives more detail on this in his book).

John's Gospel describes the packed lunch that ended up feeding 5000 men, (and possibly their wives and children which would bring the total to something like 12,000 people). How was a boy's lunch going to feed thousands of people? It seemed ludicrous! That was all the boy had. He didn't have much but what he did have, he gave to Jesus. In Jesus' Hands that lunch kept multiplying – so much so that there were 12 baskets of leftovers! Do you know that lunch is still multiplying? Even today, multitudes of people around the world will be encouraged by that boy's lunch. Every time you read John 6:1-14, you are being fed by it.

That lunch was not insignificant. Your life is not insignificant - quite the opposite. If a small packed lunch can impact nations for eternity, imagine what the ability in you can do in God's Hands. Stop looking at what you don't have. Give what *you have* for God's service instead. He will make up for any weakness or lack on your part with His strength.

Frank Jenner didn't claim to know a whole lot about the Bible. Once Jesus is your personal Lord and Saviour, you know enough to save multitudes! Many times, people who ask questions like, "What about the children in Africa?" aren't interested in the answers. This may not be the case every time, but in my experience it has been the case in the vast majority of times. It is good to grow in knowledge and to study how to answer, and indeed, to attend evangelism classes. However, don't let a fear of not knowing how to answer every question you get asked, stop you from obeying the "go" command.

Nowadays, rather than letting the person I am talking to control the conversation with questions they probably aren't interested in hearing the answers to anyway, I turn the question back on them. "What will you do with Jesus?" I ask. "That's the question you need the answer to. And the answer you give to that question will determine where you spend your eternity." Jesus told us we have to be as wise as serpents and innocent as doves. Love people enough to tell them truth. The Bible says that love never fails. Love is far superior to knowledge. Do you love Jesus? Then you are fully equipped to share Him with others.

He only needs our availability.

God is saying,"Whom shall I send, and who will go for Us?"

Will you go?

Like Isaiah, may our response be, "Here am I. Send me." (Isaiah 6:8)

41

# Chapter 5

## Your Story Is Your Tract

*"Come, see a Man Who has told me everything that I ever did! Can this be [is not this] the Christ? [Must not this be the Messiah, the Anointed One?]"* John 4:29 (Amplified Bible).

The woman from Samaria reached her town for the Lord by telling her story. The amazing part is she had only met Jesus that day! Straight after her encounter with Him, John 4:28, 29a tells us, "Then the woman left her water jar and went away to the town. And she began telling the people, "Come, see a Man Who has told me everything that I ever did!" " (Amplified Bible). She began to tell people about Jesus immediately!

Here are the results of this young believer's evangelism efforts. "So the people left the town and set out to go to Him." "So when the Samaritans arrived, they asked Him to remain with them, and He did stay there two days. Then many more believed in *and* adhered to *and* relied on Him because of His personal message [what He Himself said]. And they told the woman, Now we no longer believe (trust, have faith) just because of what you said; for we have heard Him ourselves [personally], and we know that He truly is the Savior of the world, *the Christ.*" John 4:40-42, (Amplified Bible).

Wow! Revival came to that town through the most unlikely of vessels! She hadn't exactly led a role model lifestyle, quite the opposite. She was well known in her community for all the wrong reasons. To minimise her contact with the townspeople, she had chosen to draw water from the well at noon, in the heat of the day when she knew most others would be sheltering from the sun.

To others, she was a sinner, someone to be shunned and avoided. To God, she was a person longing for love and acceptance. She found it in Jesus. Her encounter with Him changed her life! And she wasn't about to keep that to herself! A short time ago she had done all she could to avoid people. Here she was now, purposefully going to where she knew everyone was to tell them about Him. From the first time she met Jesus, she knew enough to reach her entire town for Christ! That my friend, is the power of your story.

Rev. 12:11 "And they overcame him because of the blood of the Lamb and because of the word of their testimony."

Probably the greatest tract you could give someone is your own story. No one can take from you that knowing Jesus and surrendering your life to Him has transformed your life. No theological or intellectual argument can deny your personal experience of this. Your story is a powerful evangelism tool.

Another plus with your own life story is that it is something you don't have to "learn." You have lived it and tasted it. You are intimately acquainted with the main character – you! Your story is one you can tell with ease and confidence. Ask the Holy Spirit to give you an opportunity to share it. This is one of those "I will answer quickly" prayers! When the opportunity opens up, grab it! Remember - the opportunity of a lifetime lasts the lifetime of the opportunity! Let your story flow from your heart. May your heart blaze as you remember the good things God has done for you. Your listener will be as much impressed by your enthusiasm as by your story. Your passion will touch hearts. The reality of what Jesus has done for you will impact lives. Your story will leave its mark.

Some other ways to get your story "out there" are to write it out or make a CD, about ten to fifteen minutes long, with you relating how you became a Christian. (One church I know is preparing CDs with people telling how they came to know the Lord, which they are going to hand out.) You may want to share this somewhere in your story. It is an explanation of salvation that I heard Bill Wiese give (Author of 23 Minutes in Hell). Imagine a stranger going to a nice neighbourhood and knocking on the door of a well established house. When the owner of the home answers the door, the stranger says, "I've come to live in your house." What do you think the house owner is going to say? I think the first question on his lips would be, "Who are you?" No matter how "good living" this stranger is, it wouldn't make any difference to that house owner. He doesn't know the person standing at his door and therefore, he definitely will not be coming to live with him! Many people treat salvation this way. They think their good works entitle them to a place in God's Kingdom. But salvation is not about how good you are, it is about relationship with Jesus.

If you are going to hand out written versions of your redemption story, a way to prepare would be to write or type it. This exercise also serves a dual purpose. You will have a written as well as a verbal version prepared. Having a few typed copies of your story available in your bag or pocket is an excellent way of sowing seed. Where you may be uncomfortable at first to speak about what God has done for you - you can easily hand someone a printed version your story.

If you don't type or have access to a computer, write it by hand first. Then get someone to type it for you. How about getting a soon-to-be-Christian friend to do it? Keep the length to one A4 page with the font size no smaller than 12. Before you photocopy it, get at least two people who are good readers, to proof read it for you. It is a well known fact, we don't see our own mistakes. We truly need each other!

You may also want to write a longer, more detailed version for family members, friends and acquaintances. This several page version is a profitable tool as well when travelling on aeroplanes, particularly long distance flights, for people in hospital, nursing homes or simply as God leads. I sent my long version story to a family member. It got passed on to other family members and read out in a counselling group! Many times the written version of your life can go where you can't. Once it is written, it will be an accurate truthful repetition in other people's hands.

How to write your story:

Use simple language.

Avoid Christian terminology – words like grace, anointed, righteousness, atonement, propitiation and so on.

Keep sentences short.

Use paragraphs with an extra space between each paragraph (like the paragraphs in this booklet). A page with no paragraphs is off putting and is less likely to be read.

Be honest.

Plan and write your story as follows;

Life before you became a Christian
How you were introduced to the message of Jesus
How you responded to that message
Life now as a Christian

If you feel you need help with this, talk to someone who could help you or who could perhaps suggest someone who could write it for you.

Once your story is written, include a paragraph giving your readers opportunity to surrender to Christ. If you have to, use the other side of the A4 page. It could look like this;

*Do you want to become a Christian? If so pray this prayer from your heart;*

*Lord Jesus, I believe You died for me. I believe You were raised up from the dead. I surrender my life to You today. From this day on, You only are my Lord and my Saviour. Thank You for loving me. Amen.*

Include a line encouraging your reader to contact your church if they have surrendered their life to Jesus. Remember to put your church's contact details clearly on the page.

Make several good quality photocopies. Carry copies with you as you go about your daily business. The only thing left to do is pray and give them away!

On a street outreach our church was conducting in Bangor, we were having one-on-one conversations with people about Jesus, praying for the sick and handing out tracts and invitations to our miracle service that was scheduled for later on that week. I went to give a tract to a local council worker who was picking up litter along the street where we were witnessing. He responded by saying, "Thank you, but I already have a whole load of them," and he showed me his litter bag which was full of the same tracts we had just handed out! That prompted us to take action. We decided that from then on we would pray over anything we handed out. Now before we go, we place our hands over the pile of literature we will be sowing into people's lives that day. We thank God that not one tract will fall to the ground; that each tract and leaflet will be read multiple times; that people will be queuing up to get a tract from us and that these same tracts will even go to the nations. Do you know that since we started doing that, we haven't been able to find one tract that has been thrown away when we are evangelising? People, even in groups, have come up to us and asked us if they could have a tract. And I believe that even as you read this, tracts that we have handed to people are being posted and emailed to the nations to be read there by hungry hearts. God answers prayer!

I have been on several outreaches over the years and this has always been a problem – the litter trail in the wake of a witnessing event. Now however, it is no longer a problem for us, all because of a simple prayer. Even this afternoon, before we went out, we again prayed over the literature. We handed out 400 leaflets and flyers. How many did we find that people had thrown away? None! Pray before you go out, pray that God will lead you to the right people or person and that the literature you give them will be read multiple times, reach the nations and result in salvations. Believe that each tract will be passed through entire families; that uncles, aunts, cousins, nephews, nieces, fathers, mothers, sons, daughters, husbands, wives, grandparents, and extended family members will read each tract. God is able.

The story of your salvation is just the beginning of God's exciting plan for your life. Watch how your life takes on increased levels of joy and purpose as you begin to share with people about what Jesus has done for you. What adventures await as you reach out!

## Chapter 6

## Ready, Steady, Go!

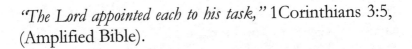

*"The Lord appointed each to his task,"* 1Corinthians 3:5, (Amplified Bible).

The Lord has appointed to each one of us a task. "What am I to do with my life? What is my calling?" This is the big question on many people's hearts. The answer is simple. Go. Go and share Jesus. This is what you are called to do. This is your appointed task. You were born to complete this assignment – to go and let your light shine in darkness.

One evening I had finished preparing dinner and it was ready to be served. My 8 year old daughter, Lois, was standing in the kitchen enjoying her new kitten. I said to her, "Can you tell the others that dinner is ready please?" She raised her voice and called in a loud voice, "DIN-EEEER IS READ-EEEEE!" "They won't hear you Lois. You will need to go and *tell* them that dinner is ready," I corrected. A few moments later, my eldest daughter Hannah arrived into the kitchen ready to eat. She had heard Lois' call. However, David, my husband didn't hear as he was too far away. It wasn't until

Hannah went and told David that dinner was ready, that he heard and came to the kitchen, ready to eat.

Does this speak to you? It certainly did to me! How many times have we called to the world from within the church, "Come. Dinner is ready." We have seen this work on occasion. Some heard, responded and came. Many didn't. Multitudes are too far away to hear. How will they hear? Only if we go. It's time to go. And it's time to go NOW. We need to go and tell them that the Lord has prepared a table for them - a table laden with goodness, mercy and loving kindness. Dinner is ready. Come and eat!

Our time here in earth is so short. You were chosen by God to be born for such a time as this. Jesus' return is imminent. It is a lot closer now than when you first believed. There are people that God has destined for you reach with a seed of His Word. What a privilege! He needs these people to be touched with His love - soon. There's an urgency to this hour. Now is a time to live with a sense of destiny like never before. It is a time unlike any other.

It's important to understand if we get so caught up in **"life as usual"** without making change and we neglect to reach out to the lost, we have missed the primary reason we are here on earth!

God has placed this booklet in your hands for a

purpose. What will you do with it? What is your decision? What action will you take?

We are all God's messengers. We are here to tell people about Jesus. Make an appointment with destiny today by taking up this challenge. Jesus came to seek and save the lost. Let His ministry to the lost continue on earth today through you. You have a significant part to play in His end time plan. You will be blessed as you go!

I am praying for you. My prayer is based on Proverbs 25:13,25. I thank God that you will be like the cold of snow in the time of harvest. You will be a faithful messenger, bringing refreshing. And as you reach out with the Word of God, it will be like water to the weary soul and good news from a distant land.

I thank God that He prospers your way as you are faithful to His call to go. And on That Day may you hear these words, "Well done, good and faithful servant. Enter into the joy of your Lord." (Matt. 25:21, NKJV).

## Thank you for reading Go!

If you have any questions, need further information or would like a version of a tract that I use when witnessing, (which you can duplicate multiple times), I would love to hear from you.

Contact me at;
Bangor Community Church, 209-211 Belfast Road,
Bangor, Co. Down, BT20 3NW,
N. Ireland

Email: siobhan@bangorcommunitychurch.co.uk

## Ordering copies of this book

It's easy to order further copies of this book, just paste the storefront link below into your browser and follow the ordering instructions: payments can be made either by credit/debit card or by PayPal.
www.lulu.com/Siobhan_Livingston

Alternatively just enter the author's name into the search textbox on Amazon's website.